INTRODUCTION

This book is not intended to be a mere list of arbitrary, albeit interesting, quotes from rich people throughout time, but rather a motivating course of action. This book is designed to make the next 365 days of your life transformative and of life-long value, with global impact.

It has been estimated that somewhere between 1 and 2 months of consistent daily activity of any kind is what builds a habit. Imagine if we focused our minds and tailored our lives around a motivating and empowering statement of truth, every day, for an entire year? Not only would you be happier, sharper, and wealthier, but the entire world would subsequently be as well.

I implore you to let your journey towards financial success and freedom begin (or continue) with this book.

HOW TO USE THIS BOOK (OTHER THAN READING IT)

I intend for this book to offer you an up-close and personal look into the minds of some of the most financially successful people throughout time. Each day, I suggest reading one quote and pondering over it throughout your day; think about it, meditate upon it, and learn how wealthy people think. Perhaps you'll become inspired with a great new business or investment strategy, or even experience a paradigm shift that leads to a journey of financial success. I wish you all the best!

DAY 1

Could I begin life again, knowing what I now know, and had money to invest, I would buy every foot of land on the Island of Manhattan.

John Jacob Astor

DAY 2

The best way to look at any business is from the standpoint of the clients

Jamie Dimon

DAY 3

I don't care what anyone says. Being rich is a good thing.

Mark Cuban

DAY 4

People are chasing cash, not happiness. When you chase money, you're going to lose. You're just going to. Even if you get the money, you're not going to be happy.

Gary Vaynerchuk

DAY 5

There are a handful of companies who understand all successful business operations come down to three basic principles; People---Product---Profit. Without top people, you cannot do much with the other two.

Malcolm Forbes

DAY 6

I learned that focus is key. Not just in your running a company, but in your personal life as well.

Tim Cook

DAY 7

I can be stressed, or tired, and I can go into a meditation and it all just flows off of me. I'll come out of it refreshed and centered and that's how I'll feel and it'll carry through the day.

Ray Dalio

DAY 8

Great companies are built on great products.

Elon Musk

DAY 9

But you are the average of the five people you associate with most, so do not underestimate the effects of your pessimistic, unambitious, or disorganized friends. If someone isn't making you stronger, they're making you weaker.

Tim Ferriss

DAY 10

Creating value isn't enough- you also need to capture some of the value you create.

Peter Thiel

DAY 11

If everyone is moving forward together, then success takes care of itself.

Henry Ford

DAY 12

Life is not fair, get used to it.

Bill Gates

DAY 13

A friendship founded on business is better than a business founded on friendship.

John D. Rockefeller

DAY 14

For me life is continuously being hungry. The meaning of life is not simply to exist, to survive, but to move ahead, to go up, to achieve, to conquer.

Arnold Schwarzenegger

DAY 15

There is only one boss. The customer. And he can fire everybody in the company from the chairman on down, simply by spending his money somewhere else.

Sam Walton

DAY 16

Think of it this way: If you got a flat tire, what would you do? Change the tire? Or get out of the car and slash the other three tires? No! Get back on the road. Don't dwell on it; don't beat yourself up. That gets you nowhere.

Jillian Michaels

DAY 17

The employer generally gets the employees he deserves.

J. Paul Getty

DAY 18

Money is my military, each dollar a soldier. I never send my money into battle unprepared and undefended. I send it to conquer and take currency prisoner and bring it back to me.

Kevin O'Leary

DAY 19

The way to become rich is to put all your eggs in one basket and then watch that basket.

Andrew Carnegie

DAY 20

Hasten slowly.

Augustus Caesar

DAY 21

Profitability is coming from productivity, efficiency, management, austerity, and the way to manage the business.

Carlos Slim

DAY 22

You don't learn to walk by following rules. You learn by doing, and by falling over.

Richard Branson

DAY 23

Sometimes by losing a battle you find a new way to win the war.

Donald Trump

DAY 24

My job is to help more people have jobs.

Jack Ma

DAY 25

All events of wealth are precluded by process, a backstory of trial, risk, hard work, and sacrifice. If you try to skip process, you'll never experience events.

MJ DeMarco

DAY 26

Taking care of your employees is extremely important and very, very visible.

Larry Ellison

DAY 27

I've been making products for so long, I have a gut feel for what is right - what will work and what won't. I can tell instantly if it's a hero or a zero.

Lori Grenier

DAY 28

I have always served the public to the best of my ability. Why? Because, like every other man, it is to my interest to do so.

Cornelius Vanderbilt

DAY 29

A brand for a company is like a reputation for a person. You earn reputation by trying to do hard things well.

Jeff Bezos

DAY 30

Capitalism cannot cause a financial crisis because capitalism is about markets constantly correcting errors. It is government intervention that can and often does cause crises.

John Tamny

DAY 31

No matter where you are in life, you'll save a lot of time by not worrying too much about what other people think about you. The earlier in your life that you can learn that, the easier the rest of it will be.

Sophia Amoruso

DAY 32

There is no substitute for hard work.

Thomas Edison

DAY 33

The joy is in the getting there. The beginning years of starting your business, the camaraderie when you're in the pit together, are the best years of your life. So rather than being so focused on when you get big and powerful, if you can just get the juice out of that... don't miss it.

Barbara Corcoran

DAY 34

Usually, you can figure out where a person's mistakes came from if you ask them the genesis of their thought process: 'Why did you do it this way?' As opposed to telling them they did it the wrong way. Understanding their thought process will ultimately help you be able to communicate with them and navigate around them.

Marcus Lemonis

DAY 35

Where there is no struggle, there is no strength.

Oprah Winfrey

DAY 36

Founding a company is hard. Most of it isn't smooth. You'll have to make very hard decisions. You have to fire a few people. Therefore, if you don't believe in your mission, giving up is easy. The majority of founders give up. But the best founders don't give up.

Mark Zuckerberg

DAY 37

Simplicity is hard to build, easy to use, and hard to charge for. Complexity is easy to build, hard to use, and easy to charge for.

Chris Sacca

DAY 38

Patience, persistence and perspiration make an unbeatable combination for success.

Napoleon Hill

DAY 39

Hustle is simple - it's doing the work. A lot of people like to talk about it, a lot of people have ideas, but it's difficult to actually do the work.

Troy Carter

DAY 40

Enjoy your sweat because hard work doesn't guarantee success, but without it you don't have a chance.

Alex Rodriguez

DAY 41

I've always been very driven and knew that to get where I wanted to go, I could never give up.

Diane Hendricks

DAY 42

Predicting rain doesn't count. Building arks does.

Warren Buffett

DAY 43

Align yourself with the right people, forge the right relationships and you'll set yourself up for the long run.

Daymond John

DAY 44

Ambition is your inner voice that tells you you can and should strive to go beyond your circumstances or station in life.

Lloyd Blankfein

DAY 45

If I complain about a traffic jam, I have no one to blame but myself.

Steve Wynn

DAY 46

In the short run, the market is a voting machine but in the long run, it is a weighing machine.

Benjamin Graham

DAY 47

Don't be intimidated by what you don't know. That can be your greatest strength and ensure that you do things differently from everyone else.

Sara Blakely

DAY 48

Any foundation you build, if trust is part of that foundation, whatever you're building, whatever you're creating is gonna have a rock-solid foundation.

Steve Tische

DAY 49

Business is a sprint until you find an opportunity, then it's the patience of a marathon runner.

Robert Herjavec

DAY 50

I truly don't believe in regret.

Bethenny Frankel

DAY 51

The biggest hurdle is rejection. Any business you start, be ready for it. The difference between successful people and unsuccessful people is that successful people do all the things the unsuccessful people don't want to do. When 10 doors are slammed in your face, go to door number 11 enthusiastically, with a smile on your face.

John Paul DeJoria

DAY 52

If you wish a thing done, get someone to do it for you; but if you wish it done well, do it yourself.

John Jacob Astor

DAY 53

It's great that people get together and collaborate, talk about the facts and the analysis, all in the interest of having a great financial system.

Jamie Dimon

DAY 54

Leaders don't look backwards to condemn what has already been done; they look forward to create a better future.

Mark Cuban

DAY 55

When I hear people debate the ROI of social media it makes me remember why so many businesses fail. Most businesses are not playing the marathon. They're playing the sprint. They're not worried about lifetime value and retention. They're worried about short-term goals.

Gary Vaynerchuk

DAY 56

Anyone who says businessmen deal in facts, not fiction, has never read old five-year projections.

Malcolm Forbes

DAY 57

Our goal has never been to make the most. It's always been to make the best.

Tim Cook

DAY 58

There are two main drivers of asset class returns - inflation and growth.

Ray Dalio

DAY 59

If you get up in the morning and think the future is going to be better, it is a bright day. Otherwise, it's not.

Elon Musk

DAY 60

A person's success in life can usually be measured by the number of uncomfortable conversations he or she is willing to have.

Tim Ferriss

DAY 61

If I had known how hard it would be to do something new, particularly in the payments industry, I would never have started

PayPal. That's why nobody with long experience in banking had done it. You needed to be naive enough to think that new things could be done.

Peter Thiel

DAY 62

If money is your hope for independence you will never have it. The only real security that a man will have in this world is a reserve of knowledge, experience, and ability.

Henry Ford

DAY 63

Research shows that there is only half as much variation in student achievement between schools as there is among classrooms in the same school. If you want your child to get the best education possible, it is actually more important to get him assigned to a great teacher than to a great school.

Bill Gates

DAY 64

You can't connect the dots looking forward; you can only connect them looking backwards. So you have to trust that the dots will somehow connect in your future. You have to trust in something - your gut, destiny, life, karma, whatever. This approach has never let me down, and it has made all the difference in my life.

Steve Jobs

DAY 65

The person who starts out simply with the idea of getting rich won't succeed; you must have a larger ambition.

John D. Rockefeller

DAY 66

Help others and give something back. I guarantee you will discover that while public service improves the lives and the world around you, its greatest reward is the enrichment and new meaning it will bring your own life.

Arnold Schwarzenegger

DAY 67

The goal as a company is to have customer service that is not just the best, but legendary.

Sam Walton

DAY 68

Life has a way of working out the way it's meant to.

Jillian Michaels

DAY 69

Money is like manure. You have to spread it around or it smells.

J. Paul Getty

DAY 70

I don't mind rude people. I want people that I can make money with, so if their executional abilities are good, and they're arrogant and rude, I don't care.

Kevin O'Leary

DAY 71

There is little success where there is little laughter.

Andrew Carnegie

DAY 72

Practice, the master of
all things.

Augustus Caesar

DAY 73

I've always said that the better off you are, the more responsibility you have for helping others. Just as I think it's important to run companies well, with a close eye to the bottom line, I think you have to use your entrepreneurial experience to make corporate philanthropy effective.

Carlos Slim

DAY 74

Fun is one of the most important - and underrated - ingredients in any successful venture. If you're not having fun, then it's probably time to call it quits and try something else.

Richard Branson

DAY 75

You should learn from your competitor, but never copy. Copy and you die.

Jack Ma

DAY 76

Many people want to change their life, but they are not willing to change their choices, and ultimately this changes nothing.

MJ DeMarco

DAY 77

I have had all of the disadvantages required for success.

Larry Ellison

DAY 78

I prefer to like the people I invest in, but it's not an absolute necessity, as long as they have a good mind and I know they'll do whatever it takes to be successful.

Lori Greiner

DAY 79

I have been insane on the subject of moneymaking all my life.

Cornelius Vanderbilt

DAY 80

We see our customers as invited guests to a party, and we are the hosts. It's our job every day to make every important aspect of the customer experience a little bit better.

Jeff Bezos

DAY 81

An economy robbed of failure is also robbed of success, because failure provides knowledge about how to succeed. Failure is the healthy process whereby a poorly run entity is deprived of the ability to do more economic harm.

John Tamny

DAY 82

Nothing will teach you more about perceived value than taking something with literally no value and selling it in the auction format. It teaches you the beauty and power of presentation, and how you can make magic out of nothing.

Sophia Amoruso

DAY 83

Many of life's failures are people who did not realize how close they were to success when they gave up.

Thomas Edison

DAY 84

In business, you're the Chief Salesman. Create a sense of demand, rather than waiting to have demand.

Barbara Corcoran

DAY 85

People are the core of every business. Businesses are based on relationships, and relationships are based on people. I would go to an average restaurant run by amazing people over an outstanding restaurant run by awful people.

Marcus Lemonis

DAY 86

Doing the best at this moment puts you in the best place for the next moment.

Oprah Winfrey

DAY 87

Facebook was not originally created to be a company. It was built to accomplish a social mission - to make the world more open and connected.

Mark Zuckerberg

DAY 88

A great idea can't succeed without a great operator. But rarely can a great operator squeak by with a bad idea. So, as pithy as it sounds to say 'It's all about the people,' I only invest when I think I have found the right team for the right business.

Chris Sacca

DAY 89

Education comes from within; you get it by struggle and effort and thought.

Napoleon Hill

DAY 90

Coming from the music business and seeing the transition from artists to fans, fans to consumers, it's really about understanding the psychology of why people want to associate with your brand.

Troy Carter

DAY 91

Winners live in the present tense. People who come up short are consumed with future or past. I want to be living in the now.

Alex Rodriguez

DAY 92

Talk to successful entrepreneurs. Learn about what they've experienced so you can avoid some of the pitfalls that come with wealth.

Diane Hendricks

DAY 93

Price is what you pay. Value is what you get.

Warren Buffett

DAY 94

An entrepreneur must pitch a potential investor for what the company is worth as well as sell the dream on how much of a profit can be made.

Daymond John

DAY 95

Businesses will ultimately go where the markets and opportunities are.

Lloyd Blankfein

DAY 96

Money doesn't make people happy. People make people happy.

Steve Wynn

DAY 97

The intelligent investor is a realist who sells to optimists and buys from pessimists.

Benjamin Graham

DAY 98

I failed the LSAT. Basically, if I had not failed, I'd have been a lawyer and there would be no Spanx. I think failure is nothing more than life's way of nudging you that you are off course. My attitude to failure is not attached to outcome, but in not trying. It is liberating.

Sara Blakely

DAY 99

I would say I'm an optimist by nature.

Steve Tisch

DAY 100

Oh, I'm all about small business. I think what we've learned from big business and big Wall Street is that unchecked greed and the creation of false value gets us all in trouble. If we look at the American economy, who's really creating value? It's the small businesses.

Robert Herjavec

DAY 101

You cannot show people only the petals and not the thorns. It's not fair to them.

Bethenny Frankel

DAY 102

Success unshared is failure.

John Paul DeJoria

DAY 103

The only thing standing between you and your goal is the bullshit story you keep telling yourself as to why you can't achieve it.

Jordan Belfort

DAY 104

Very true, but now you shall see what I will do with this money. With eight thousand dollars I buy eighty lots above Canal Street. By the time your lot is worth twelve thousand dollars, my eighty lots will be worth eighty thousand dollars.

John Jacob Astor

DAY 105

I'm a little bit of an eternal optimist. People always say to me, 'If you go do this and it fails, what are you going to do?' I don't care. I'm going to give it my best shot. That's what I'm going to do. If it doesn't work, it doesn't work. And I'll try again.

Jamie Dimon

DAY 106

If you can't admit a failure, you're not an entrepreneur. You are not a good business person. There's nothing brilliant about what you are doing.

Mark Cuban

DAY 107

What's money? A man is a success if he gets up in the morning and goes to bed at night and in between does what he wants to do.

Bob Dylan

DAY 108

Stop doing things that waste time. Don't replace time with your family or things that you need to do. I needed to put together two fantasy teams this weekend because that's something I enjoy, but I did stop playing Nintendo Wii for hours on end.

Gary Vaynerchuk

DAY 109

Success follows doing what you want to do. There is no other way to be successful.

Malcolm Forbes

DAY 110

Think about what you're passionate about. I did not learn something early enough: if I could go back, I'd tell the younger me that there's a big difference between loving to work and loving the work.

Tim Cook

DAY 111

Over the long run, the price of gold approximates the total amount of money in circulation divided by the size of the gold stock. If the market price of gold moves a long way from this level, it may indicate a buying or selling opportunity.

Ray Dalio

DAY 112

The path to the CEO's office should not be through the CFO's office, and it should not be through the marketing department. It needs to be through engineering and design.

Elon Musk

DAY 113

$1,000,000 in the bank isn't the fantasy. The fantasy is the lifestyle of complete freedom it supposedly allows.

Tim Ferriss

DAY 114

The next Bill Gates will not start an operating system. The next Larry Page won't start a search engine. The next Mark Zuckerberg won't start a social network company. If you are copying these people, you are not learning from them.

Peter Thiel

DAY 115

Before everything else, getting ready is the secret of success.

Henry Ford

DAY 116

You may have heard of Black Friday and Cyber Monday. There's another day you might want to know about: Giving Tuesday. The idea is pretty straightforward. On the Tuesday after Thanksgiving, shoppers take a break from their gift-buying and donate what they can to charity.

Bill Gates

DAY 117

For the past 33 years, I have looked in the mirror every morning and asked myself: 'If today were the last day of my life, would I want to do what I am about to do today?' And whenever the answer has been 'No' for too many days in a row, I know I need to change something.

Steve Jobs

DAY 118

I know of nothing more despicable and pathetic than a man who devotes all the hours of the waking day to the making of money for money's sake.

John D. Rockefeller

DAY 119

Failure is not an option. Everyone has to succeed.

Arnold Schwarzenegger

DAY 120

Control your expenses better than your competition. This is where you can always find the competitive advantage.

Sam Walton

DAY 121

It's important in life to celebrate any victory in life.

Jillian Michaels

DAY 122

The man who comes up with a means for doing or producing almost anything better, faster or more economically has his future and his fortune at his fingertips.

J. Paul Getty

DAY 123

Working 24 hours a day isn't enough anymore. You have to be willing to sacrifice everything to be successful, including your personal life, your family life, maybe more. If people think it's any less, they're wrong, and they will fail.

Kevin O'Leary

DAY 124

The average person puts only 25% of his energy and ability into his work. The world takes off its hat to those who put in more than 50% of their capacity and stands on its head for those few and far between souls who devote 100%.

Andrew Carnegie

DAY 125

Only that which is well done is quickly done.

Augustus Caesar

DAY 126

You don't need to raise taxes on rich people, because they create capitalization and investment. But you need to tax speculation - meaning capital gains.

Carlos Slim

DAY 127

One thing is certain in business. You and everyone around you will make mistakes.

Richard Branson

DAY 128

What separates the winners from the losers is how a person reacts to each new twist of fate.

Donald Trump

DAY 129

The lessons I learned from the dark days at Alibaba are that you've got to make your team have value, innovation, and vision. Also, if you don't give up, you still have a chance. And, when you are small, you have to be very focused and rely on your brain, not your strength.

Jack Ma

DAY 130

Stop giving a shit what anyone else says, thinks, or writes — unless they are your market and/or your customers.

MJ DeMarco

DAY 131

I believe people have to follow their dreams - I did.

Larry Ellison

DAY 132

There is no such thing as failure. There are only results.

Tony Robbins

DAY 133

I had a history for starting something and maybe getting halfway done. Then I'd see the same thing I was doing on the bestseller list! My ideas were right, but I hadn't done them fast enough.

Lori Greiner

DAY 134

If I had learned education I would not have had time.

Cornelius Vanderbilt

DAY 135

You know you're not anonymous on our site. We're greeting you by name, showing you past purchases, to the degree that you can arrange to have transparency combined with an explanation of what the consumer benefit is.

Jeff Bezos

DAY 136

Most people do not begin life on top. Politicians who raise income tax rates on top earners in the name of "fairness" are telling the strivers lower down that they will incur a penalty for succeeding.

John Tamny

DAY 137

I believe that there is a silver lining in everything, and once you begin to see it, you'll need sunglasses to combat the glare.

Sophia Amoruso

DAY 138

Someone is sitting in the shade today because someone planted a tree a long time ago.

Warren Buffett

DAY 139

Being busy does not always mean real work. The object of all work is production or accomplishment and to either of these ends there must be forethought, system, planning, intelligence, and honest purpose, as well as perspiration. Seeming to do is not doing.

Thomas Edison

DAY 140

The best time to expand is when people are asleep at the wheel.

Barbara Corcoran

DAY 141

Put no more than three messages on a lemonade stand. You have to describe what your product is, why it's the best, and how much it is. Don't be drawing turtles and flowers and footballs all over it, distracting people. Keep it clean.

Marcus Lemonis

DAY 142

When you think about growing and being empowered yourself, it is what you've been able to do for other people that leaves you the fullest.

Oprah Winfrey

DAY 143

When you give everyone a voice and give people power, the system usually ends up in a really good place. So, what we view our role as, is giving people that power.

Mark Zuckerberg

DAY 144

Effective storytelling is the key to getting users to understand and adopt your product as well as imperative to recruiting team members and future investors.

Chris Sacca

DAY 145

Action is the real measure of intelligence.

Napoleon Hill

DAY 146

It isn't that every company is going to be successful. The law of averages shows that 80% of companies are going to fail.

Troy Carter

DAY 147

I've always enjoyed challenges.

Alex Rodriguez

DAY 148

I don't think I have ever taken any 'offbeat' advice. Actually, I don't know if I take any advice very often. I trust my own instincts and seek out information so I can make fully informed decisions. That's what's worked for me.

Diane Hendricks

DAY 149

The investor of today does not profit from yesterday's growth.

Warren Buffett

DAY 150

No matter what business you're in, business is business, and financing and money are critical. I would have made a lot fewer mistakes if I had more schooling in that area.

Daymond John

DAY 151

With interest rates rising, gold doesn't pay an interest rate, but every other currency - it becomes not only less important to hold gold as an alternative, but more expensive to hold it as an insurance policy and so that will be a burden on the price of gold.

Lloyd Blankfein

DAY 152

Keeping customers is about the experience, and the employees control the culture and temperature of the business. Never forget that.

Steve Wynn

DAY 153

There is no man living that can not do more than he thinks he can.

Henry Ford

DAY 154

Give me a stock clerk with a goal, and I will give you a man who will make history. Give me a man without a goal, and I will give you a stock clerk.

J.C. Penny

DAY 155

Most of the time common stocks are subject to irrational and excessive price fluctuations in both directions as the consequence of the ingrained tendency of most people to speculate or gamble... to give way to hope, fear and greed.

Benjamin Graham

DAY 156

It's the power of the brand. We've never formally advertised.

Sara Blakely

DAY 157

Success… seems to be connected with action. Successful people keep moving. They make mistakes, but they don't quit.

Conrad Hilton

DAY 158

The idea of getting a lifetime job, and making $100,000 a year, with benefits, is dead and gone. It's over. And it may never come again. That's a very scary thought for a lot of people.

Robert Herjavec

DAY 159

My recipes aren't geared towards women; my books are marketed towards women because women are the biggest market for weight loss, weight management and weight maintenance and for cooking.

Bethenny Frankel

DAY 160

I could go insane if I obsessed over every little detail of all of my companies. My management philosophy is to pay attention to the vital few and ignore the trivial many.

John Paul DeJoria

DAY 161

Act as if! Act as if you're a wealthy man, rich already, and then you'll surely become rich. Act as if you have unmatched confidence and then people will surely have confidence in you. Act as if you have unmatched experience and then people will follow your advice. And act as if you are already a tremendous success, and as sure as I stand here today - you will become successful.

Jordan Belfort

DAY 162

When an economist says the evidence is "mixed," he or she means that theory says one thing and data says the opposite.

Richard Thaler

DAY 163

You know what it's like to wake up in the middle of the night with a vivid dream? And you know that if you don't have a pencil and pad by the bed, it will be completely gone by the next morning. Sometimes it's important to wake up and stop dreaming. When a really great dream shows up, grab it.

Larry Page

DAY 164

Scale can create value for shareholders; for consumers, who are beneficiaries of better products, delivered more quickly and at less cost; for the businesses that are our customers; and for the economy as a whole.

Jamie Dimon

DAY 165

I'm a competitive person. Business is a much more competitive sport than any real sport. It's 24x7x365. I'm a business adrenaline junky.

Mark Cuban

DAY 166

Too many people spend money they earned to buy things they don't need to impress people they don't like.

Will Rogers

DAY 167

There is only one class in the community that thinks more about money than the rich, and that is the poor.

Oscar Wilde

DAY 168

Never spend your money before you have it.

Thomas Jefferson

DAY 169

Money is only a tool. It will take you wherever you wish, bit it will not replace you as the driver.

Ayn Rand

DAY 170

If all the economists were laid end to end, they'd never reach a conclusion.

George Bernard Shaw

DAY 171

Money is a terrible master but an excellent servant.

P.T. Barnum

DAY 172

Empty pockets never held anyone back. Only empty heads and empty hearts can do that.

Norman Vincent Peale

DAY 173

I will tell you the secret to getting rich on Wall Street. You try to be greedy when others are fearful. And you try to be fearful when others are greedy.

Warren Buffett

DAY 174

Demand is best measured in terms of spending. You know, I think in traditional economics, it's a mistake to measure it in terms of the quantity of goods.

Ray Dalio

DAY 175

If everybody is doing it one way, there's a good chance you can find your niche by going exactly in the opposite direction.

Sam Walton

DAY 176

Be reactionary. React to what the market wants. And the market wants one-on-one real time engagement. Now that we have the tools to engage, I'm going to continue fighting for the end user.

Gary Vaynerchuk

DAY 177

I have met many entrepreneurs who have the passion and even the work ethic to succeed - but who are so obsessed with an idea that they don't see its obvious flaws. Think about that. If you can't even acknowledge your failures, how can you cut the rope and move on?

Kevin O'Leary

DAY 178

If I ever took a business public, I wouldn't want to take the shares off the table. I don't want people thinking I'm doing it just to make money and then going to run for the hills. I think that's a very important distinction.

Marcus Lemonis

DAY 179

Luck is a product of process, action, work, and being 'out there.' And when you're out there, you stand the right chance at being in the right place at the right time.

MJ DeMarco

DAY 180

Investors must keep in mind that there's a difference between a good company and a good stock. After all, you can buy a good car but pay too much for it.

Richard Thaler

DAY 181

Let me issue and control a nation's money and I care not who writes the laws.

Mayer Amschel Rothschild

DAY 182

I will stand up for what I believe and for what I have always believed: Every person has a right to be rich in this country and I want to help them get there.

Jim Cramer

DAY 183

Owning a great golf course gives you great power.

Donald Trump

DAY 184

Real estate investing, even on a very small scale, remains a tried and true means of building an individual's cash flow and wealth.

Robert Kiyosaki

DAY 185

We recruit our people for personality. We look for the people person, with innate warmth, sweetness, and intelligence. These are the people who are sending your message out to the customers and potential customers, so we recruit for personality first and foremost.

Steve Wynn

DAY 186

The glow of one warm thought is to me worth more than money.

Thomas Jefferson

DAY 187

Someone is out there looking to put you out of business. Someone is out there who thinks they have a better idea than you have. A better solution than you have. A better or more efficient product than you have.

Mark Cuban

DAY 188

The likelihood of success drops dramatically when you expand, especially in the services business. And there's a lot of capital that goes into opening another office.

Marcus Lemonis

DAY 189

A good name is rather to be chosen than riches.

King Solomon

DAY 190

The reason we love our parents is because they loved us first. Every single company should take this advice.

Gary Vaynerchuk

DAY 191

If your customer base is aging with you, then eventually you are going to become obsolete or irrelevant. You need to be constantly figuring out who are your new customers and what are you doing to stay forever young.

Jeff Bezos

DAY 192

Millionaire wealth has nothing to do with the stock market, it has nothing to do with clipping coupons, and it has nothing to do with a great job and a 401(k).

MJ DeMarco

DAY 193

Money is a gift from God.

Paul Solomon

DAY 194

If you don't like the idea that most of the money spent on lottery tickets supports government programs, you should know that most of the earnings from mutual funds support investment advisors' and mutual fund managers' retirement.

Robert Kiyosaki

DAY 195

It's fine to celebrate success but it is more important to heed the lessons of failure.

Bill Gates

DAY 196

An entrepreneur needs to know what they need, period. Then they need to find an investor who can build off whatever their weaknesses are - whether that's through money, strategic partnerships or knowledge.

Daymond John

DAY 197

The mutual fund industry provided the money for Intel and Motorola and Hewlett-Packard to crush the competitors.

Jim Cramer

DAY 198

It's not that we can predict bubbles - if we could, we would be rich. But we can certainly have a bubble warning system.

Richard Thaler

DAY 199

You should have more time for you during all of your life - not when you're 65 and retired.

Carlos Slim

DAY 200

The only reason to do business is to make money; that's the only reason for doing business.

Kevin O'Leary

DAY 201

The real tragedy of the poor is the poverty of their aspirations.

Adam Smith

DAY 202

Taxes are not good things, but if you want services, somebody's got to pay for them so they're a necessary evil.

Michael Bloomberg

DAY 203

Crony capitalism is essentially a condition in which... public officials are giving favors to people in the private sector in payment of political favors.

Alan Greenspan

DAY 204

A corporation's primary goal is to make money. Government's primary role is to take a big chunk of that money and give it to others.

Larry Ellison

DAY 205

Unemployment insurance is a pre-paid vacation for freeloaders.

Ronald Reagan

DAY 206

The men who have succeeded are men who have chosen one line and stuck to it.

Andrew Carnegie

DAY 207

When you've got 10,000 people trying to do the same thing, why would you want to be number 10,001?

Mark Cuban

DAY 208

All money is a matter of belief.

Adam Smith

DAY 209

There's a reason why start-ups, especially disruptive start-ups - like Google or Amazon or Uber - are full of young people. That's because young people are not as wedded to the old fashioned ways of doing things.

Richard Thaler

DAY 210

Successful investing is anticipating the anticipations of others.

John Maynard Keynes

DAY 211

Nobody likes being around poor people, especially poor people.

Steve Wynn

DAY 212

I had to pick myself up and get on with it, do it all over again, only even better this time.

Sam Walton

DAY 213

If you want to take control over your life and freedom-filled millionaire track, you need to start your own business, one that you can control and leverage by virtue of your own good decisions and hard work.

MJ DeMarco

DAY 214

Assets put money in your pocket, whether you work or not, and liabilities take money from your pocket.

Robert Kiyosaki

DAY 215

Imagine if you had baseball cards that showed all the performance stats. You could see what they did well and poorly and call on the right people to play the right positions in a very transparent way.

Ray Dalio

DAY 216

I have ways of making money that you know nothing of.

John D. Rockefeller

DAY 217

Successful people are 100% convinced that they are masters of their own destiny, they're not creatures of circumstance, they create circumstance, if the circumstances around them suck they change them.

Jordan Belfort

DAY 218

No complaint... is more common than that of a scarcity of money.

Adam Smith

DAY 219

The biggest misconception about work is that you need to spend the majority of your time doing it.

Tim Ferriss

DAY 220

You're either humble or you're not. If you were a jerk before the fame, you just become a jerk with a bigger spotlight. Whoever you are really comes through.

Oprah Winfrey

DAY 221

Part of what made the Macintosh great was that the people working on it were musicians, poets, and artists, and zoologists, and historians. They also happened to be the best computer scientists in the world. But if it hadn't been computer science, these people would have been doing amazing things in other fields.

Steve Jobs

DAY 222

A good leader doesn't get stuck behind a desk.

Richard Branson

DAY 223

Life is hard, and a lot of people come home tired from work. If they're gonna spend half an hour reading, they want some entertainment and a sense of achievement. So that's what I give them. That's all I'm trying to do. Is that really so wrong?

James Patterson

DAY 224

I believe the returns on investment in the poor are just as exciting as successes achieved in the business arena, and they are even more meaningful!

Bill Gates

DAY 225

Derivatives are financial weapons of mass destruction.

Warren Buffett

DAY 226

You can't run a business just by selling one thing.

Marcus Lemonis

DAY 227

And I think the more money you put in people's hands, the more they will spend. And if they don't spend it, they invest it. And investing it is another way of creating jobs. It puts money into mutual funds or other kinds of banks that can go out and make loans, and we need to do that.

Michael Bloomberg

DAY 228

A stock is not just a ticker symbol or an electronic blip; it is an ownership interest in an actual business, with an underlying value that does not depend on its share price.

Benjamin Graham

DAY 229

Stop saying, 'I wish.'
Start saying, 'I will.

MJ DeMarco

DAY 230

Nobody wants to buy a $60,000 electric Civic. But people will pay $90,000 for an electric sports car.

Elon Musk

DAY 231

Other people's successes are good news - for them and for you. Good for you because they show you a way to go.

Steve Wynn

DAY 232

Winners use words that say 'must' and 'will'.

Jordan Belfort

DAY 233

I do not understand where the backing of Bitcoin is coming from. There is no fundamental issue of capabilities of repaying it in anything which is universally acceptable, which is either intrinsic value of the currency or the credit or trust of the individual who is issuing the money, whether it's a government or an individual.

Alan Greenspan

DAY 234

Look at what caused people to make a lot of money and you will see that usually it is in proportion to their production of what the society wanted.

Ray Dalio

DAY 235

If Wal-Mart invests a billion dollars and others invest $100 million, Wal-Mart is going to grow more.

Carlos Slim

DAY 236

Don't blame the marketing department. The buck stops with the chief executive.

John D. Rockefeller

DAY 237

I had no idea that being your authentic self could make me as rich as I've become. If I had, I'd have done it a lot earlier.

Oprah Winfrey

DAY 238

The secret of your success is determined by your daily agenda.

John C. Maxwell

DAY 239

Your college degree doesn't signify education; it signifies brainwashing. Your education doesn't end at graduation, it begins. The sooner you learn that all the skills you need to succeed will occur after you leave the confines of educational conformation. The sooner you will succeed.

MJ DeMarco

DAY 240

If the reason people invest is to make money, then in seeking advice they are asking others to tell them how to make money. That idea has some element of naïveté.

Benjamin Graham

DAY 241

Move fast and break things. Unless you are breaking stuff, you are not moving fast enough.

Mark Zuckerberg

DAY 242

When I come to work each day, whether as a commentator for TheStreet.com or a host of Mad Money With Jim Cramer, I have only one thought in mind: helping people with their money.

Jim Cramer

DAY 243

One of my rules for investing is, I don't invest in a deal where I don't think I have an unfair advantage and where I don't think I can personally impact the outcome.

Chris Sacca

DAY 244

Well done is better than well said.

Benjamin Franklin

DAY 245

In the '30s, the Keynesian stuff worked at least in the sense that you could print money without inflation because there was all this productivity growth happening. That's not going to work today.

Peter Thiel

DAY 246

All you can do is the best you can do.

Lloyd Blankfein

DAY 247

The idea that everyone should slavishly work so they do something inefficiently so they keep their job - that just doesn't make any sense to me. That can't be the right answer.

Larry Page

DAY 248

Being flooded with information doesn't mean we have the right information or that we're in touch with the right people.

Bill Gates

DAY 249

When your desires are strong enough you will appear to possess superhuman powers to achieve.

Napoleon Hill

DAY 250

Surplus wealth is a sacred trust which its possessor is bound to administer in his lifetime for the good of the community.

Andrew Carnegie

DAY 251

Only buy something that you'd be perfectly happy to hold if the market shut down for 10 years.

Warren Buffett

DAY 252

When something is important enough, you do it even if the odds are not in your favor.

Elon Musk

DAY 253

I'm really not a great businessperson. I understand business, and I understand numbers, but I think what I understand more than that is people... Ultimately, I think businesses fail and people fail because they don't have their act together.

Marcus Lemonis

DAY 254

Money equals freedom.

Kevin O'Leary

DAY 255

Learn to say 'no' to the good so you can say 'yes' to the best.

John C. Maxwell

DAY 256

I think it's very important to have a feedback loop, where you're constantly thinking about what you've done and how you could be doing it better. I think that's the single best piece of advice: constantly think about how you could be doing things better and questioning yourself.

Elon Musk

DAY 257

Obvious prospects for physical growth in a business do not translate into obvious profits for investors.

Benjamin Graham

DAY 258

The ultimate definition of insanity is to prostitute your Monday through Friday for the paycheck of Saturday and Sunday.

MJ DeMarco

DAY 259

Without action, the best intentions in the world are nothing more than that: intentions.

Jordan Belfort

DAY 260

When looking at trends I always ask myself basic and timeless questions about business, and the one I seem to always come back to is, 'How is this different than anything else in the marketplace?'

Daymond John

DAY 261

The reason I was able to grow my business was that every day, after producing 30 minutes of wine television, I spent 15 hours a day replying to every single person's e-mail and every single person's Twitter @ reply.

Gary Vaynerchuk

DAY 262

After military service, the most patriotic thing you can do as a wealthy person is pay your taxes.

Mark Cuban

DAY 263

The way to get started is to quit talking and begin doing.

Walt Disney

DAY 264

It's only when the markets are perceived to have exhausted themselves on the downside that they turn. Trying to prevent them from going down just merely prolongs the agony.

Alan Greenspan

DAY 265

I began playing Monopoly for real when I was 26 years old. Today, my wife and I have approximately 1,400 little green houses - each paying us monthly. You do not have to be a rocket scientist or have a Harvard degree to play Monopoly for real.

Robert Kiyosaki

DAY 266

College gives people learning and also takes away future opportunities by loading the next generation down with debt.

Peter Thiel

DAY 267

Innovation has nothing to do with how many R & D dollars you have. When Apple came up with the Mac, IBM was spending at least 100 times more on R & D. It's not about money. It's about the people you have, how you're led, and how much you get it.

Steve Jobs

DAY 268

It is not by augmenting the capital of the country, but by rendering a greater part of that capital active and productive than would otherwise be so, that the most judicious operations of banking can increase the industry of the country.

Adam Smith

DAY 269

Invest only if you would be comfortable owning a stock even if you had no way of knowing its daily share price.

Benjamin Graham

DAY 270

If I earn a million dollars a week and the average American earns a thousand dollars a week, then when I spend twenty thousand dollars on something it's the equivalent of the average American spending twenty dollars on something, right?

Jordan Belfort

DAY 271

I attract a crowd, not because I'm an extrovert or I'm over the top or I'm oozing with charisma. It's because I care.

Gary Vaynerchuk

DAY 272

People care about what your business can do for them. How will it help them? What's in it for them? Will it solve their problem? Make their life easier?

MJ DeMarco

DAY 273

You should set goals beyond your reach so you always have something to live for.

Ted Turner

DAY 274

Failed plans should not be interpreted as a failed vision. Visions don't change, they are only refined. Plans rarely stay the same and are scrapped or adjusted as needed. Be stubborn about the vision, but flexible with your plan.

John C. Maxwell

DAY 275

If your access to health care involves your leaving work and driving somewhere and parking and waiting for a long time, that's not going to promote healthiness.

Larry Page

DAY 276

I think it's fair to say that personal computers have become the most empowering tool we've ever created. They're tools of communication, they're tools of creativity, and they can be shaped by their user.

Bill Gates

DAY 277

A goal is a dream with a deadline.

Napoleon Hill

DAY 278

Credit is an 'I love debt' score.

Dave Ramsey

DAY 279

Observing is really the fuel to innovating, ultimately.

Mark Parker

DAY 280

It seems like the right thing to do is tackle problems other people aren't working on.

Sean Parker

DAY 281

Luck is a dividend of sweat. The more you sweat, the luckier you get.

Ray Kroc

DAY 282

People are going to copy your product if you build great stuff. Just because Yahoo has a search box doesn't make it Google.

Evan Spiegel

DAY 283

Because if you're prepared and you know what it takes, it's not a risk. You just have to figure out how to get there. There is always a way to get there.

Mark Cuban

DAY 284

You could own the best hotel in the world located on the best beach in California, but if customers are treated like inconveniences and requests go unfulfilled, they won't return.

MJ DeMarco

DAY 285

Companies that grow create wealth. This, in turn, allows people to have jobs that create more growth and more wealth. It's a virtuous cycle.

Lloyd Blankfein

DAY 286

If you want to succeed you should strike out on new paths, rather than travel the worn paths of accepted success.

John D. Rockefeller

DAY 287

I think good private equity investors create a lot more economic value than they destroy.

Bill Ackamn

DAY 288

Both poker and investing are games of incomplete information. You have a certain set of facts and you are looking for situations where you have an edge, whether the edge is psychological or statistical.

David Einhorn

DAY 289

Don't go in and tell somebody else how to run their business.

Carl Icahn

DAY 290

You have to learn the rules of the game. And then you have to play better than anyone else.

Unknown

DAY 291

Teamwork makes the dream work, but a vision becomes a nightmare when the leader has a big dream and a bad team.

John C. Maxwell

DAY 292

You can never quit. Winners never quit, and quitters never win.

Ted Turner

DAY 293

Here is a guiding principle: If a business collects data on consumers electronically, it should provide them with a version of that data that is easy to download and export to another Web site.

Richard Thaler

DAY 294

If I could set a world record, it would be that I have 150 business partners, all with thriving businesses of their own that started with nothing and I made the difference to make them all billionaires.

Barbara Corcoran

DAY 295

An investment operation is one which, upon thorough analysis promises safety of principal and an adequate return. Operations not meeting these requirements are speculative.

Benjamin Graham

DAY 296

All money means to me is a pride in accomplishment.

Ray Kroc

DAY 297

You make more money if you're generous.

Robert Kiyosaki

DAY 298

I believe that if you show people the problems and you show them the solutions they will be moved to act.

Bill Gates

DAY 299

My favorite things in life don't cost any money. It's really clear that the most precious resource we all have is time.

Steve Jobs

DAY 300

If you have to think about "affordability," you can't afford it because affordability carries conditions and consequences.

MJ DeMarco

DAY 301

Poverty was the greatest motivating factor in my life.

Jimmy Dean

DAY 302

It's not about working harder; it's about working the system.

Evan Spiegel

DAY 303

You simply have to put one foot in front of the other and keep going. Put blinders on and plow right ahead.

George Lucas

DAY 304

There's a way to do it better- find it.

Thomas Edison

DAY 305

Do the one thing you think you cannot do. Fail at it. Try again. Do better the second time. The only people who never tumble are those who never mount the high wire. This is your moment. Own it.

Oprah Winfrey

DAY 306

You can't build a reputation on what you are going to do.

Henry Ford

DAY 307

This is what you need to do in a luxury business: look for people who will like being there every day.

Steve Wynn

DAY 308

It is so much easier to be nice, to be respectful, to put yourself in your customers' shoes and try to understand how you might help them before they ask for help, than it is to try to mend a broken customer relationship.

Mark Cuban

DAY 309

The easiest way to make money is -create something of such value that everybody wants and go out and give and create value, the money comes automatically.

Jordan Belfort

DAY 310

Money was never a big motivation for me, except as a way to keep score. The real excitement is playing the game.

Donald Trump

DAY 311

I feel that luck is preparation meeting opportunity.

Oprah Winfrey

DAY 312

The man who acquires the ability to take full possession of his own mind may take possession of anything else to which he is justly entitled.

Andrew Carnegie

DAY 313

I don't create companies for the sake of creating companies, but to get things done.

Elon Musk

DAY 314

Millions of Americans and people around the world, especially young people who face intense financial challenges today, haven't been taught how to take control of their financial future.

Robert Kiyosaki

DAY 315

I love what I do. I don't do it for the money. I work on behalf of investors that I like and want to do well for. I'm a competitive person.

Bill Ackman

DAY 316

Every technological revolution takes about 50 years.

Jack Ma

DAY 317

Running a start-up is like eating glass. You just start to like the taste of your own blood.

Sean Parker

DAY 318

This is a great time for the 'guerilla marketer.' The days when you used to have to buy expensive TV time and a yellow page ad to get started are gone.

Dave Ramsey

DAY 319

As a leader, the first person I need to lead is me. The first person that I should try to change is me.

John C. Maxwell

DAY 320

When growth is slower-than-expected, stocks go down. When inflation is higher-than-expected, bonds go down. When inflation is lower-than-expected, bonds go up.

Ray Dalio

DAY 321

The global recession has exposed the Slowlane for the fraud it is. With no job, the plan fails. When the stock market loses 50% of your savings, the plan fails. When a housing crisis erases 40% of your illiquid net worth in one year, the plan fails. The plan is a failure because the plan is based on time and factors you can't control. Unfortunately, millions of people have faithfully invested decades into the plan only to discover the ugly truth: The Slowlane is risky and insufferably impotent.

MJ DeMarco

DAY 322

All you have in business is your reputation - so it's very important that you keep your word.

Richard Branson

DAY 323

The sad truth is that many behavioral economists know very little about psychology.

Richard Thaler

DAY 324

I enjoy the hunt much more than the 'good life' after the victory.

Carl Icahn

DAY 325

Every man has his price, or a guy like me couldn't exist.

Howard Hughes

DAY 326

The single biggest financial mistake I've made was not thinking big enough. I encourage you to go for more than a million. There is no shortage of money on this planet, only a shortage of people thinking big enough.

Grant Cardone

DAY 327

Your big opportunity may be right where you are now.

Napoleon Hill

DAY 328

It's basically impossible to teach someone if they aren't curious about the subject. This is where modern schooling goes wrong.

Tai Lopez

DAY 329

I'd like to create a space for people who have a lot of talent but not a lot of reach.

Evan Spiegel

DAY 330

99.5 percent of the people that walk around and say they are a social media expert or guru are clowns. We are going to live through a devastating social media bubble.

Gary Vaynerchuk

DAY 331

I'm a big fan of all-you-can-eat plans, because they're simpler for customers.

Jeff Bezos

DAY 332

Our philosophy is that we care about people first.

Mark Zuckerberg

DAY 333

Success comes to those who have an entire mountain of gold that they continually mine, not those who find one nugget and try to live on it for fifty years.

John C. Maxwell

DAY 334

The goal is not comfort, it is freedom!

Grant Cardone

DAY 335

Make a list of the people you admire and what makes them amazing. Then go out and become those things yourself.

Tai Lopez

DAY 336

Microsoft could help Facebook with one of the biggest challenges, namely monetizing its traffic without reducing the user's experience. It's obvious that Microsoft needs traffic and Facebook needs search.

David Einhorn

DAY 337

The man who does more than he is paid for will soon be paid for more than he does.

Napoleon Hill

DAY 338

If we did all the things we are capable of, we would literally astound ourselves.

Thomas Edison

DAY 339

The rich are those who play to win. The middle class plays not to lose.

Robert Kiyosaki

DAY 340

The theory that can absorb the greatest number of facts, and persist in doing so, generation after generation, through all changes of opinion and detail, is the one that must rule all observation.

Adam Smith

DAY 341

There's a profound difference between interest and commitment. Interest reads a book; commitment applies the book 50 times.

MJ DeMarco

DAY 342

If you're not a risk taker, you should get the hell out of business.

Ray Kroc

DAY 343

I'm not a micromanager.
I don't believe in that.

Mark Parker

DAY 344

The best entrepreneurs I've ever met are all good communicators. It's perhaps one of the very few unifying factors.

Tim Ferriss

DAY 345

Never sacrifice physical health in the pursuit of money. That's a given. Figure out a strategy to raise both simultaneously. It's tricky.

Tai Lopez

DAY 346

Headlines, in a way, are what mislead you because bad news is a headline, and gradual improvement is not.

Bill Gates

DAY 347

You won't get much done if you only grind on the days you feel good.

Grant Cardone

DAY 348

We can change our lives. We can do, have, and be exactly what we wish.

Tony Robbins

DAY 349

A market is never saturated with a good product, but it is very quickly saturated with a bad one.

Henry Ford

DAY 350

When a well-packaged web of lies has been sold gradually to the masses over generations, the truth will seem utterly preposterous and its speaker a raving lunatic.

MJ DeMarco

DAY 351

Constantly probe the people who report to you and encourage them to probe you.

Ray Dalio

DAY 352

The space between failure and success seems large. It's not. The difference between a good carpenter and a bad one is about a quarter of an inch.

Tai Lopez

DAY 353

My organization, my colleagues and I, are paid to run hotels in good times and fair times. We're professionals. That's what we do. I don't give a damn about the short-term market implications.

Steve Wynn

DAY 354

One person seeking glory doesn't accomplish very much.

Sam Walton

DAY 355

If we were motivated by money, we would have sold the company a long time ago and ended up on a beach.

Larry Page

DAY 356

I don't want to disrupt anything. We never conceive of our products as disruptive - we don't look at something and say, 'Let's disrupt that.' It's always about how we can evolve this and make this better.

Evan Spiegel

DAY 357

Cherish your visions and your dreams as they are the children of your soul, the blueprints of your ultimate achievements.

Napoleon Hill

DAY 358

Fast is the new big. Perfection is the killer to production. Perfection is basically a symptom of procrastination.

Grant Cardone

DAY 359

Historically, privacy was almost implicit, because it was hard to find and gather information. But in the digital world, whether it's digital cameras or satellites or just what you click on, we need to have more explicit rules - not just for governments but for private companies.

Bill Gates

DAY 360

To create real wealth, make someone else wealthy first. This is the law of the mentor/apprentice.

Tai Lopez

DAY 361

If you want to be successful, find someone who has achieved the results you want and copy what they do and you'll achieve the same results.

Tony Robbins

DAY 362

You cannot push any one up a ladder unless he be willing to climb a little himself.

Andrew Carnegie

DAY 363

The more we turn down questionable offers like trip insurance and scrutinize 'one month' trials, the less incentive companies will have to use such schemes.

Richard Thaler

DAY 364

In school, failure is a bad thing. Marked by a bloody F and a parental beatdown, failure is admonished. Fail and you're grounded! No TV, no iPad! Is it any shock that straight-A students make great employees while the C-students are the guys hiring them? The A-students do as they're told, follow rules unquestioningly and stay within the lines. Meanwhile, C-student and future billionaire Johnny is a ninth grader's newest BFF—he's underneath the bleachers selling his older brother's Playboys at twenty-five dollars a pop.

MJ DeMarco

DAY 365

Income inequality in a capitalist system is truly beautiful. It provides the incentive for creative people to gamble on new ideas, and it turns luxuries into common goods. Income inequality nurses sick companies back to health. It rewards hard work, talent, and achievement regardless of pedigree. And it's a signal that some of the world's worst problems will disappear in our lifetimes.

John Tamny

FINAL THOUGHTS

Even just writing this book has been an incredibly easy and motivating experience for me. I truly hope that you have derived great benefit from the statements throughout. Thank you for reading and I hope you live a long, strong, happy, and ultimately prosperous life; because when you are motivated and inspired, others become motivated and inspired, and that makes the world a better place for all of us!

Bryan James

2018